# LETTERS TO GRANDPA

### by Patrick D. Goran

### 2022

*Patrick Goran*

If you have any questions, visit **www.letters2grandpa.com**

First paperback edition October 2022

Second paperback "Blossom Ridge" edition December 2022

Editing by Patrick D. Goran and Deb Stanley

Layout by Patrick D. Goran and Maegan Sadocha

The original images featured in this book were produced by the author.

ISBN 9798359234221 (Paperback)

Published by Kindle Direct Publishing

**www.letters2grandpa.com**

This book is dedicated to my Grandma

SANDRA KAY GORAN

September 23, 1935 – March 12, 2021

And my Grandpa, who both lived their fullest lives at Blossom Ridge and Blossom Springs, in Rochester Hills, Michigan. This was due to the lasting friendships made with the wonderful residents, the dedication of the kind staff, and the great vision and generosity of the Moceri family. Thank you.

# Great Times At Blossom Ridge

# Cover

The picture featured on the back cover was taken on February 27th, 2021 at The Jagged Fork in Rochester Hills, Michigan. It is a picture of me, in front of a stack of delicious S'mores French Toast. I was very excited that day because I would see my grandma, who I had not hugged in over a year due to the COVID-19 pandemic. It would be one of the last times I saw her.

# Contents

# Preface

I was so excited to see my Grandma! It had been over a year now and I was not able to see her due to the Covid-19 restrictions. When we arrived, she seemed very happy. She had been living with her dementia for over nine years now and she usually didn't talk much. The disease had started gradually. She would occasionally forget our names or ages, but her dementia progressively worsened until she barely spoke. Occasionally she would utter a quiet "Yeah" if we asked her a question, but she didn't talk much other than that.

We pushed Grandma around the assisted living center in her wheelchair, and for the first time in a year, I got to see her smile. She loved people, even though she couldn't remember them. She loved the energy of conversation and human interaction. Everything seemed perfect that day and every time I said her name she rewarded me with her beaming smile. Unfortunately, this would be the last time I would see her smile.

Early on a Wednesday, my brother and I were abruptly pulled out of school to see Grandma. She was connected to an oxygen machine, and the sound of her labored breathing echoed in the room. It was crazy to think that just 13 days ago, she was so happy and now she was unable to move, barely able to breathe. The family members gathered around her, noses red and throats dry, as we knew this would be the last time we would see her. I took hold of her hand and I told her something important, that we would always love her, and we left her room for the last time. Later that night she died peacefully in her sleep. I will never forget her smile and her warm personality and the mark that she left on the world.

Her death affected everyone deeply, especially Grandpa. For years, Grandpa had taken close care of her needs, helping her into bed, helping her when she fell, helping her eat, until it became too much for him. She would often wake up in the night, not knowing where she was, not knowing what to do. As things continued to get worse, both of them moved into an assisted living center. Through it all, Grandpa was there to comfort her. At times he seemed a little distant from us because he was so focused on Grandma's care, but I didn't blame him. Although he was tired, he was always doing his best when Grandma needed him most.

I was inspired to write these letters as a way to reconnect with my Grandpa and remind him that there are so many things in life to discover, despite Grandma's passing. I wanted to share things with him from my perspective. The discussions we have had after reading these letters have been magical and have led to a deeper friendship with my Grandpa. I hope these letters inspire you and become a source for reflection and discussion along life's journey. I love you so much Grandpa! Enjoy the letters.

# Nature

*Admire this great world that we have been given and enjoy every moment of nature's beauty.*

Dear Grandpa,

Hi! It's Patrick. This is my first letter. I am very excited to start this project and I can't wait to start writing to you! Today we are going to talk about nature. Nature is an absolutely beautiful thing. I mean, look outside. It is truly magical: the trees, the water, the animals that live in both. Look at the squirrels as they scurry across the grass and into the trees, and watch the spiders meticulously build their webs, as they are beautifully decorated by the morning dew drops. See the birds chirp, fly, and dive throughout the sky. This is the true magic of nature.

Nature consists not only of the animals and trees we see, but also the things that we don't see. For instance, wind makes up an important part of nature, even though we can't see it. We can see the effects of wind, but we can never truly see the wind. In fact, often the most important aspects of life we can't even see, but we can always appreciate. Nature has not only made things just right to support us, but it also has the power to destroy with hurricanes, earthquakes, and tsunamis. This is also the beauty of nature; its power makes it divine, and even in destruction, its actions are renewing and pure.

I love water. When I am in it, it feels like I am floating in the air, like flying. As long as I can hold my breath, I fly and I look at the green plants on the bottom of the lake and rocks pushed up through the soft sand. I fly through the water kicking my legs as the surface becomes farther and farther away. The endless blue surrounds me and I am engulfed in nature.

So, I encourage you to go outside and take a walk. Admire this great world that we have been given and enjoy every moment of nature's beauty. It might reveal something in yourself you never knew was there.

# Time

*Time is a gift, not a consequence, despite what others might say.*

Dear Grandpa,

Today I am going to talk about time. Now, many people think that growing, especially growing older, is a consequence, a slow punishment of sorts. In reality, it is a blessing. Time helps us reflect on ourselves and to see how we can improve. If we had unlimited time, we wouldn't cherish it; we wouldn't be driven to remember the moments that were special to us. Time is a gift, not a consequence, despite what others might say.

Why is it, that as we grow older, time seems to be slipping out of our reach, going like a speeding car that will never stop until it reaches its destination? When we want it to go slowly, it goes fast, and when we want it to go fast, it moves slowly, like it is trying to work against us. We scream directions from the backseat, but the car turns randomly, disregarding our plea. We have all experienced that feeling. When we are doing something boring, time seems to go by so slowly, but when we are doing something fun, it always slips away faster than it should. Even though time may seem inescapable, there is a way to fight against it.

Cherish every moment, fun or boring, and you will find that time will pass by at a more manageable pace. Life and time are a tremendous gift. We may never fully understand its curves, peaks and valleys, but we can live in the now, and cherish every moment for what it is. We can see the beauty in everyone and everything, and maybe, just maybe, enjoy our time a little bit more. Because time is not infinite, but our ability to love is.

# Inspiration

*The world is so full of ideas and things that are really unique, and I try to use that to my advantage*

Dear Grandpa,

Today we are going to talk about inspiration. Inspiration is amazing and I use it a lot in my writing. I find a lot of my inspiration comes from the world around us. The world is so full of ideas and things that are really unique, and I try to use that to my advantage. My inspiration also comes from when I am trying to fall asleep. Before I go to sleep, I reflect upon the day and its events and new ideas pop into my head. I always have sticky notes beside my bed so I can easily grab one and write down an idea to use in my stories. My inspiration also comes from my dreams. I dream of so many things. When I wake up, I remember what happened, and I incorporate those adventures and experiences into my writing.

Inspiration can also be uplifting, like being inspired to say a kind word, or thinking of something fun to do with a new friend. Finding this kind of inspiration can help others, even if we may not realize it. Being inspired to say hello or thank you, or saying something nice to someone who is going through a difficult time, can help someone feel appreciated and can have a significant impact on them. Our inspiration and ideas can affect the people around us. I hope these letters affect you in a positive way, as they have affected me.

So, I encourage you, before you go to sleep, reflect on the day that is coming to an end and think about how you can improve the next day and be more kind and loving to other people. The impact your reflections will have, not only on you, but on others, will be unimaginable.

# Acceptance

*Learning from our mistakes helps us to keep moving forward, and loss can teach us many valuable lessons.*

Dear Grandpa,

Today we are going to talk about acceptance, specifically acceptance of the past. This is a difficult topic, but it is essential. Our lives are built on habits. When we wake up in the morning, what do we do? Do we eat breakfast? Do we watch TV? Or do we reflect on the day ahead? These are all habits we develop over time, and through our habits we can see why the past is so powerful. At times the past can appear to tell us who we are and who we will become. So, don't linger on the past and let it control your destiny.

Sometimes the past holds secrets we don't want to reveal, or mistakes we regret making. Sometimes it holds sorrow, like losing the life of a loved one. These things can affect our emotions and how we react to situations, but we shouldn't let them completely control us. Learning from our mistakes helps us to keep moving forward, and loss can teach us many valuable lessons. It is hard, but seeing the good in life's situations, even our mistakes, can help us a lot. My brother is especially good at this; he always manages to see the good in everything, even when we are talking about something serious. If we dwell on loss and don't move forward, it can be confining, and can affect us negatively.

I know the loss of Grandma has been hard on you, and we will remember her as the wonderful and great person she was, but if she was here, she would tell us to have some fun and enjoy life, because we only get to live once. Grandma loved all of us and we love her back. She will always be with us; we just have to remember that truth as we move forward.

I imagine life as a spinning wheel; it goes forward and we move with it and remember where we've been. Loss is hard and it can take a toll on us, but if we don't move forward, it can take an even bigger toll on us. Life is a wheel, and moving with it until the road of life ends, is as essential as the unfolding road itself.

# Fear

*Face your fears, especially the ones that affect you the most, and you will find they are probably not as bad as you thought, and you will have conquered a fear.*

Dear Grandpa,

Today, we are going to talk about fear, specifically, how to overcome it. Now, fear is a hard thing to deal with. We are all afraid of something, and sometimes fear feels like it consumes us and dictates our actions, but it doesn't have to. It is important to face our fears and try to conquer them, because they can become barriers that keep us from enjoying our lives. Sometimes, we are afraid we will have to face a certain situation, a certain mistake, or even a certain emotion. This hinders us and doesn't allow us to move forward. It is like we are faced with a brick wall and given only a spoon. Almost everyone has one or two irrational fears that can affect them every day. I have a fear of needles so I hate getting shots, but I always get through them, and they are never as bad as my mind makes them out to be.

Some people grow out of their fears, but others sadly, don't. Instead, their fears linger and take hold of them. Only we can decide how to embrace our own fears. Do we ignore them, try to live with them, or do we try to overcome them? A great way to move past our fears is to face them head-on. In doing so, we will probably realize that they aren't so bad. I used to have a fear of spiders, but gradually that fear is going away. I am less and less afraid of them because I have had exposure to them. I see them outside and I don't think they are scary. I actually admire them. They spend hours building their beautiful webs, and catch pesky bugs with them too! Face your fears, especially the ones that affect you the most, and you will find they are probably not as bad as you thought, and you will have conquered a fear. The feeling is priceless. Afterwards, you will probably wonder why you were so afraid of it in the first place. You will shrug and go on with the rest of your life, having overcome a fear that hindered you once before, and you will find yourself relieved that it does not have any control over you anymore.

Fear is hard, but it helps us stay focused, so we can move past it and find freedom from its grip. With enough time, your spoon will break through the brick wall and you will be set free.

# Waking up & Falling Asleep

*One decision can change everything. One choice has the power to change our lives forever, as well as the lives of those around us.*

Dear Grandpa,

Today we are going to talk about waking up and falling asleep. Waking up is a wondrous thing. It represents the infinite amount of choices a new day presents. When we wake up, we are replenished and energized and ready to start the new day. This feeling is amazing because each day holds many possibilities, good and bad. We, as individuals, make thousands of decisions every day, and those decisions have a ripple effect, not only on one day, but over the course of our lives. One decision can change everything. One choice has the power to change our lives forever, as well as the lives of those around us. Waking up is the symbol of the infinite possibilities that come with the vastness of each new day.

Falling asleep represents reflection. Before I fall asleep, I think of the choices I made during the day, and try to think what I could do if I ran into that situation again. Before going to sleep, we should reflect on our day. We can ask ourselves questions, such as: Was I trying to be myself today? Did I make good choices? What bad decisions did I make? How did my actions impact those around me? How could I improve my decisions tomorrow? These simple questions can improve our outlook on life, as well as our future choices.

These reasons are why waking up and falling asleep are so special. We are given the opportunity to reflect upon ourselves and what we do, so we can improve. That is the glory of self-reflection; if we embrace it, it will be a blessing to us, as well as to all the wonderful people around us.

# Life

*No matter where life takes us, or what it presents us, we can be forever grateful for the present moment.*

Dear Grandpa,

Today we are going to talk about life. Life is quite an adventure! There are ups and downs and twists and turns, and within them all, moments that make us laugh, smile, and cry. Many people go through life looking only forward, because they assume it will be better there. I often hear people say, "I will do this when I have this; I will be happy when l accomplish this; when I have that, then I will be happy." Well, the truth is that if we only look forward to things we can never truly experience the gifts of the present. Don't get me wrong; it is nice to look forward to fun things and it is okay to do so, but if we never stop to experience the now, we can get stuck in a vicious loop of want and desire. I should know because sometimes I do this with my writing! "I'll write when I buy this. I'll write after I do this." It seems almost impossible to combat!

One of the ways to help ourselves live in the present is to be with people we love, like friends and family. Go do an activity with them or just talk and listen to them. This is a good way to experience the present because it distracts us from looking into the future. It breaks the loop, even if it's just for a little while, and allows us to be in the moment, and maybe have some fun. We always seem to be looking towards the destination, when we really need to learn to enjoy the journey. Life can be challenging at times and can present us with things we do not expect, but if we learn to find happiness in these moments, then we can enjoy life to its fullest. No matter where life takes us, or what it presents us, we can be forever grateful for the present moment.

Don't wait until you get that thing you want, or until you feel like it. Start now, because the truth is, there will always be a reason to hesitate. We should learn to enjoy what we have now. So take action. Do that thing you've always wanted to do and enjoy it! Do it with the time and resources you have today because you may not be given another opportunity tomorrow.

That is the adventure of life. It's unpredictable, it's amazing, and may feel downright crazy at times, but it is an adventure. Enjoying our journey, and going on it with the people we love, is just as important, if not more so, than the final destination.

# Friendship

*Friendship is an essential part of our everyday lives. Friendship builds trust, understanding, and sometimes, even leads to love*

Dear Grandpa,

Today, we are going to talk about friendship. Friendship is a wonderful thing that is happening all around us. When we are friends with someone, we look out for them and care for them. We are willing to be there for them when they need us, help them emotionally and physically, and maybe even lay down our life for them. We feel a bond with that person, a connection, and we care about their well-being and their life. That is what friendship is, and the bonds of friendship are limitless.

Friendship is the basis of a lot of things we observe around us. Countries are built on friendship, borders are created when sometimes friendships are not found, and war compels soldiers to fight for their country and their friends, with the danger of death looming. Even the bond of marriage is a product of deep friendship. Friendship is an essential part of our everyday lives. Friendship builds trust, understanding, and sometimes, even leads to love.

Unfortunately, sometimes friendships are pulled apart, whether it's the result of distance, disagreements, or even death. Friendships don't always last forever, but they can always be remembered. When we become friends with someone they become a part of us, like a part of our family. That is why it is so hard to let go of them. When we let go, a piece of ourselves remains with them.

Life is hard, but we persevere through the heartbreaks, the hardships, and the sorrows. We live on and continue, because we know life is just around the corner, waiting to show us something new, and maybe even spark another friendship that can last a lifetime. Life is about seeing these moments for the opportunities that they are and taking hold of them, because life is unpredictable and even sometimes insane. But, we only live once, and only we can choose who we share our magic moments with.

# Hobbies

*The feeling of gaining inspiration, and then creating something unique, is truly a blessing.*

Dear Grandpa,

Today we are going to talk about hobbies, specifically, hobbies where we create something. I think that it is important to have a hobby. Hobbies are something we can rely on when we need them, whether it is to pass the time, let out some bottled-up emotions, or just to relax. For example, writing is one of my favorite hobbies. I enjoy it, and I like that I create something when I'm finished, whether it's the letter I am writing you now, a short story, or maybe even a novel. I feel a need to create stories and to share them with others, to try to stimulate emotions out of words on a page. It seems almost silly at first that someone could care so much about letters of ink on a piece of paper, but as writers, we want the readers to feel a connection to the characters, like they are actual people.

I think hobbies can help us as individuals to express ourselves, whether it's painting, drawing, writing, or even knitting. These activities can help us show our true colors, literally, while creating something original in the process. The feeling of gaining inspiration, and then creating something unique, is truly a blessing. You look at it and know it's yours. You own it. You created it. That feeling of creating is so amazing and beautiful to me! When I read back my writing, I try to see what I can improve and what I can do better next time. We can do this with almost anything in life when we create something.

Hobbies help us express things in ourselves we never knew were there, and to experience our lives in a fun and enjoyable way. This is the importance of a hobby. I hope that you can continue an old hobby, or maybe try a new one, because hobbies are a way to explore our uniqueness and our emotions in ways we never thought possible.

# Routine

*So, I encourage you to try to be flexible, while also upholding a routine, because only then can you have mastery over yourself, your routine, and ultimately your happiness.*

Dear Grandpa,

Today we are going to talk about routine. Routine is a great thing. Knowing what we're going to do can provide us with stability and confidence. Routine acts as a guide and helps us to be organized and efficient throughout our day when moving from one task to the next. As important as routine is, after a while we can become slaves to our routines. What do I mean by that? Sometimes we can become trapped in our routines and they can lead us further from our dreams.

It is important to find the right balance between routine and flexibility because having a balance between the two is an essential ingredient for living a purposeful life. Many people lean toward either the rigid side or the flexible side, but balance is key. When we are too flexible we may feel like we have no direction, but when we are too rigid we may feel like our habits are a prison, isolating us from friends, family, and even our dreams. There are severe consequences awaiting both extremes.

To help achieve this balance, I try to have certain chunks of my day scheduled, while leaving other times open for the unexpected. This allows the schedule and routine to be a guide, while also leaving time for flexibility and balance. Ultimately, it's up to each one of us to find the best approach to balance routine and flexibility, allowing our happiness to flourish. This balance usually exists, not in the extremes, but rather within the movement between them.

So, I encourage you to try to be flexible, while also upholding a routine, because only then can you have mastery over yourself, your routine, and ultimately your happiness. Because that's what we all crave isn't it? Having a healthy grasp of this can help us better embrace the everyday, as well as the unexpected surprises that we will encounter along life's journey.

# Keys to Happiness

*When some people see a mystery, they see it as something that can be solved with a definitive answer, but this is a different kind of mystery.*

Dear Grandpa,

Today we are going to talk about the keys to happiness. This is a very interesting topic because it is a mystery. What are the keys to happiness? I certainly don't know them yet and some people look their whole lives to try to find the keys to happiness, but sadly never succeed. They try everything they can to be happy and to find their happiness, and yet, it still eludes them. On the other hand, some individuals don't look at all, and just go through life. They may even find one of the keys, but are too blind to see it.

     None of these ways is wrong, I just think they are overlooking a critical point. When some people see a mystery, they see it as something that can be solved with a definitive answer, but this is a different kind of mystery. It is not a mystery to be solved, but instead is one to be discovered over a lifetime. It is so big and so vast that some might never find the answer, but what is even more puzzling, is that two people who think they have found the keys will often have differing answers.

     This mystery is one that does not lead to one single answer, because happiness is as complex as the people who seek it. Only you can uncover this mystery. Only you can find your own answer; no one else can do it for you. But the question is, do you choose to look, or will you do nothing at all? The keys to happiness may never be fully known, but we can still discover our own keys to happiness while walking our path of self-discovery.

# Magic Moments

*These moments are usually the most unexpected; that is why they make the biggest impact.*

Dear Grandpa,

Today we are going to talk about magic moments. These moments are somewhat unexplainable, but they trigger something within the mind that makes that moment special to us. These moments are usually the most unexpected; that is why they make the biggest impact. Sometimes the simplest actions trigger them. Whether it is a conversation with a loved one, a first kiss, or a beautiful sunset, these moments are completely unique to us.

These magic moments act as mental guideposts for us to follow. When we feel sad or lonely, we can bring back these joyful memories to help us feel better. When we feel overwhelmed or uncertain, we can remember that these memories are something that bring comfort. When we feel alone in the world, these memories remind us of the people in our lives who love us. That is why they are so special. They often feel chosen for us to remind us to keep moving forward and to reflect on where we have been.

We need things to guide us throughout our lives and this is one of the ways we are guided. These moments inspire us, strengthen us, and help us strive to be better. They are the things in our corner telling us to get up and fight. They are the things telling us there is still hope, and there always will be! We all have experienced at least one magical moment, and that is all we need to keep us moving forward. If we can bring that moment back into our lives, we can again experience the wisdom and inspiration found in these magic moments. One moment can guide us in life and ignite our sense of purpose, just like a single spark can light a blazing fire.

# The Treasures of Failure

*If we are too afraid of failure, we will never try, and that is a guaranteed failure.*

Dear Grandpa,

Today we are going to talk about the treasures of failure. Failure is often seen as something bad. Whether it is a failure of a project, a business, or a task, failure can be consuming, leeching our time, energy, and willpower, for seemingly no benefit, or at least that's what we can think.

We can learn extremely important things from failure, like what not to do, how to deal with failure, and how to avoid it in the future. We all hate failure, but it is essential. If we are going to fail, we should fail small, fail fast, learn from it, and keep going. We shouldn't be trapped in fear of failure, but instead, embrace it as part of the process. We often have to first lose, before we can ever truly win. If we are too afraid of failure, we will never try, and that is a guaranteed failure. Just remember, every time we fail, we grow closer to knowing the right answer.

We all need to fail in life, as a reminder that we still can. Just because something that failed took up a lot of time doesn't mean it was worthless. We need to fail faster and learn better, so that eventually we will learn the best solution, the highest response. Instead of being angry at failure, we should learn to treasure it, because failure is the coach whom we learn the most from in life, so we can continue to improve to be the best we can be.

# Life and Death

*If we lived everyday as if it were our last, I think we would all act differently.*

Dear Grandpa,

Today we are going to talk about life and death. Death is just as much a part of our lives as life. Death often hurts, especially when it involves someone we love. The feeling of someone being taken away from our lives into a different place impacts us deeply. We often feel powerless once it happens, like all that we can do is accept it and remember the person they once were.

Death enables us to reflect on life. If we never experienced death, we would never cherish life or its special moments. If someone who died could come back for only a few minutes, I think they would tell us not to let their death tear us down, but to enjoy our life while it still lasts, because we never know if we'll have tomorrow. Death is what makes life special. Our lives are finite, like a ticking clock that will end somewhere, somehow; it's just a question of when. If we lived everyday as if it were our last, I think we would all act differently. We would try to end rivalries, settle old arguments, show the people we love that we appreciate them, and try to make a difference in the world while we still can. Death makes us reflect on what we've done and what we haven't done, but we should also remember our lives are not only about death; our lives are also full of life.

Our lives are full of life through our parents, through our magic moments, through everything around us. From a baby in their parents' arms, to a bee on a flower, we are surrounded by life. Just remember, that amidst death, life carries on. Like most things in life, death can be a great teacher. It can inspire us to honor the lives and memories of our lost loved ones as spiritual and moral forces that continue to guide us ever closer toward our sacred life purpose.

# Dreams

*If we are passionate about something, we should do whatever it takes to achieve that goal.*

Dear Grandpa,

Today we are going to talk about dreams. Dreams come in all shapes and sizes and have the power to shape our lives in ways we never thought possible. Maybe our dream is to learn a challenging new skill we have not dared to try, or to depart on an exciting adventure where true love waits for us to arrive. Maybe it is to achieve one of our life's biggest goals, but it seems too impossible to achieve. The question is, do we have the courage to chase our dreams, or do we choose to not even try?

One of my dreams is to write a book, but not just any book, a book that has an impact on people and can help them change their lives for the better. I want my writings to be heard and to help people, whether it is to give them guidance from my perspective, to help them feel better during a hard time, or even as entertainment! I don't know why, but it has always been something I have desired to do. It is one of my life's biggest dreams.

Even so, I have realized it will take lots of hard work, patience, and perseverance to achieve this goal, and it will not be easy. I think this is one of the biggest reasons we often give up on our dreams. When we were in kindergarten, maybe we wanted to be an astronaut so we could venture into space, but we gave up that dream when we got older, when we realized how much training we would have to go through, and all the work it entailed. All of the memorizing and problem solving looked exhausting. Despite all of our yearnings to uphold our dream, we decided that it wasn't a foreseeable possibility.

When we grow older, our knowledge increases, especially about the world around us, and reality takes its strong hold on us. In other words, dreams often become less and less of a possibility as time passes in our lives. Maybe it's our daily responsibilities, or what family and friends say, or just not having enough courage to dream. Some might even say, "That's why they are called dreams, because you can only imagine them."

Well, to that I say, "No!" If we are passionate about something, we should do whatever it takes to achieve that goal. No matter how much work we may have to endure, if we embrace our inspired vision, we will accomplish that dream. That is the beauty of our dreams. They always have the power to challenge us and help us grow, eventually becoming the new reality in our lives.

# Freedom

*I believe it is through our daily tasks that we develop and discover those interests and talents that ultimately lead us to our divine purpose in life.*

Dear Grandpa,

Today we are going to talk about freedom. Freedom is something that every human cherishes. Being able to do what we want, when we want, to ultimately be free. Often people feel trapped by their daily obligations, whether it is going to work or waking up at a certain time. We would rather be like birds and just fly around seeing the sights from above, not responsible for any of the everyday activities we have to endure. Birds don't have to worry about house bills or the taxes!

Well, we are not birds that can fly around whenever we please; instead we are human beings, and that is much greater than being a bird. Does freedom come from the absence of these daily obligations and tasks? I believe it is through our daily tasks that we discover and develop those interests and talents that ultimately lead us to our divine purpose in life I think that is why I like writing so much. Even though it takes a lot of perseverance, and at times it can be challenging, writing allows me the freedom of thought to choose the ideas, events, and characters that go into my stories. It is through our daily responsibilities that we discover our soul work, and ultimately that is where true freedom lies.

So, enjoy those daily tasks, whether it is learning to paint, or playing a sport, or even cleaning up a room, and experience the freedom and skills that are developed through these activities. Ask yourself, "How can I joyfully immerse myself in these daily activities so I can better help those around me?" In time, something will inspire you and it may lead you closer to your life purpose. Be grateful for all those daily responsibilities and exercise the freedom of your mind, because this is the freedom we all desire. In this way, we realize that we do not need to seek freedom from the outside world, because true freedom can be discovered in every one of our decisions and actions along the path of purpose in our lives.

# Identity

*It is often the birthplace of our dreams and where change becomes possible.*

Dear Grandpa,

Today we are going to talk about identity. Identity is an important concept that has such a huge impact on the way other people view us, and how we view ourselves. Do you base your identity only on the opinions of other people? Are there any other qualities and talents that you choose not to show that make up your identity? To help answer these questions, I think it is very useful to see our identity as having two sides like a coin, the exterior identity and the interior identity.

The exterior identity is what the outside world thinks of us. How would your friends describe you in one word; adventurous, shy, funny? All of these descriptions combined become our exterior identity. Unfortunately, sometimes the mistakes that we've made in the past can become a prominent part in making up our exterior identity. This side of our identity is not even created by us, but instead is based on the perceptions of the people around us. We may find ourselves having little control over our exterior identity because its power lies in the hands of other people. If we only focus on this side of our identity, the stress can become overwhelming and our pursuits may be based on such things as, "how can I avoid embarrassment" or "how can I blend in with the crowd?"

On the flip side, our interior identity is what we think about ourselves, those things the outside world often never gets to see. Maybe other people see us as an amazing sports player, but actually our interior identity is that of a writer; but we have been keeping our stories hidden. Our interior identity is a necessary side of us because it is where we have both the control and freedom to let our imaginations run free, to learn, and to try new things before the world gets to see. It is often the birthplace of our dreams and where change becomes possible.

So, fully embrace the distinction that you have both an exterior and interior identity and see the world open up to you. Your exterior identity is not who you are, but only a current perception of a limited part of you. If people want to make up their own identities for you, let them! You don't have control over what they call you, so don't let it overshadow your interior identity. Use those parts of your exterior identity, whether accurate or not, to become the needed motivation to help propel you toward your dreams. Commit to your dreams. Nurture and share those unique and inspired parts of your interior identity so they may flourish and in time become a new part of your exterior identity. In this way you can also help inspire other people to develop their interior identity and that can make all the difference in helping make the world a better place to live.

# Belief

*They give us a friend, they distribute the weight, they give us hope.*

Dear Grandpa,

Today we are going to talk about belief. Belief is something that we cling to as human beings. Believing that we can do something, believing that everything will be okay, believing in God. We all believe, and we look towards our beliefs for guidance throughout the day, and over the course of our lives.

Belief is one of the most powerful gifts we can utilize. Belief shapes us by telling us what is possible and influences what we are willing to try. When we believe in something, we put our whole selves into it, we trust our living body to our belief, and I would go so far as to say, it takes a lot of courage to believe. We have to be brave to believe, to put our trust into something so much we are willing to even give our lives for that cause. That is belief. When we believe in someone, something, or anything, we are putting our trust in their hands, whether it is a secret given to a friend, or even ourselves in a marriage. We trust they will do the right thing with it, because we believe in them.

It may be difficult to believe and it takes courage and faith, but belief is important. We need something to look towards, we need someone to lean on. When we feel alone, when we feel the crippling weight of the world on our shoulders, when it seems there is no hope, our beliefs lift us back up. They give us a friend, they distribute the weight, they give us hope. That is what belief is, and when we believe in something with strength and conviction, we have the power to change the world for the better.

# Don't Fear the End

*Instead of fearing the end, we should embrace it, because the end is never an end; it is just a new beginning, a new door to open, a new trail to explore.*

Dear Grandpa,

Today we are going to talk about fearing the end, and specifically, why we should not be afraid of the end. The end of anything can be scary - the end of a job, the end of a relationship, the end of a life. Usually these events are linked to negative emotions, like sadness, despair, and grief. All of these feelings mixed together can create a tremendous amount of fear for the end, because these are the feelings we associate with it. We often hide from it, we distract ourselves from it, we run from it. We try to do everything in our power to not accept the hard fact that things will end.

It is okay to be scared of the end; it is only natural, but if we spend all of our energy worrying about the future, we can't fully experience the gifts of the present. Why worry about the end when it hasn't come yet? If we are so scared of the end, why not use it to inspire us to live life to the fullest while we still can? Go achieve that goal you've always wanted to achieve. Go have fun with your loved ones. Instead of fearing the end, we should embrace it, because the end is never an end; it is just a new beginning, a new door to open, a new trail to explore.

Life is breathtaking. From the moment we are conceived, our lives are filled with infinite possibilities, and this is truly magical. Most of us can taste, see, hear, smell, feel, speak, and walk. We can do all of these things, and yet we often take them for granted. Enjoy the present and don't fear the end, because we still have now and that is something we should all be grateful for.

Remember, life is a journey, and even when the journey ends, our story continues, through the people we love, the memories we have made with them, and the impact we have had on others. We will all live on in some way or another; we will all leave our mark. We will always remember Sandy. She was a great mother, a great wife, and a great grandma to me, among so many other things. Her impact will forever live on through us. We just need to remember that an end is never a true end; it is just a new beginning, a way of life showing us something new, and reminding us that there is something truly amazing awaiting us beyond the trees.

# Epilogue

I never anticipated how much these letters would impact my relationship with my Grandpa. It has been a little over a year since the passing of my grandma and we all continue to try to honor her and cherish her spirit. Grandpa is doing well and he says the letters are helping him so much. He immediately started sharing my letters with his friends, and they began to post them on their assisted living community activity board at Blossom Ridge, allowing others there to read the letters as well.

My grandpa claims that these simple passages on life have provided him with daily inspiration and healing and have been a source of many conversations that have blossomed around the breakfast and dinner tables. These letters have not only allowed me to share time with Grandpa and connect with him at a deeper level, but have also provided an avenue for him to build new friendships, while sharing memories, hardships, joy, and laughter with others in his community. I am so grateful that my writing has not only touched him, but others as well. This has been one of my biggest dreams in life, and being able to share this with my grandpa, has been a truly magical experience. It has brought me a happiness I cannot put into words.

As my grandpa shared the reactions from his community regarding my letters, I came to realize that so many people were going through similar struggles with loss, and that dementia was very common in other families as well. Worldwide, it is estimated that 50 million people suffer from dementia. In the U.S. alone, approximately 1 in 9 individuals over the age of 65 are diagnosed with this disease and about one person is being diagnosed every single minute of the day. Dementia and Alzheimer's affect countless people and have taken many loved ones away from their husbands, wives, friends, and family.

For these reasons, I will be donating a portion of the proceeds from this book to the Alzheimer's Association to help provide more resources to families impacted by this devastating disease. This organization is a global leader for both dementia research and support services and brings caregivers and families together to improve their understanding of this disease and learn better ways to cope and care for their affected loved ones. In this way, I believe my letters will continue to help others, even when these pages are not being read. It is my heartfelt wish that these letters will be a source for reflection and inspiration that will help you along life's journey. Thank you for listening, thank you for sharing, and thank you Grandpa.